HORRIBLE HISTORIES

TUDORS

A HIGH-SPEED HISTORY

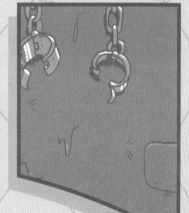

TERRY DEARY

FOR PAUL BURDESS. TD

FOR JO. 'WHO'S QUEEN?' DS

SCHOLASTIC CHILDREN'S BOOKS,
EUSTON HOUSE, 24 EVERSHOLT STREET,
LONDON NW1 1DB, UK

A DIVISION OF SCHOLASTIC LTD
LONDON ~ NEW YORK ~ TORONTO ~ SYDNEY ~ AUCKLAND
MEXICO CITY ~ NEW DELHI ~ HONG KONG

PUBLISHED IN THE UK BY SCHOLASTIC LTD, 2010

TEXT COPYRIGHT © TERRY DEARY, 2010
ILLUSTRATIONS COPYRIGHT © DAVE SMITH, 2010

ALL RIGHTS RESERVED

ISBN 978 1407 11179 7

PRINTED AND BOUND BY TIEN WAH PRESS PTE. LTD, SINGAPORE

2 4 6 8 10 9 7 5 3 1

CONTENTS

History has been going on such a long time. There is so much history your brain can't fit it all in. Let me show you...

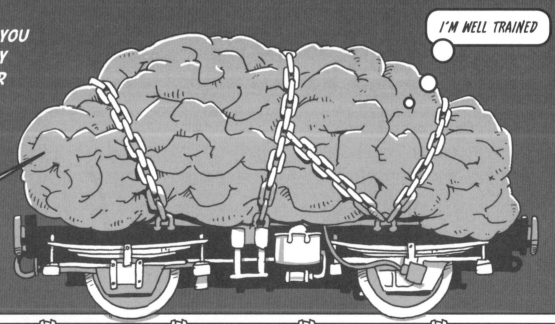

SO WHAT WE NEED IS HISTORY IN SMALLER BITS. YOU MAY WANT TO KNOW ALL ABOUT THE TERRIFYING TUDORS. NOW YOU JUST NEED A CAR TO CARRY YOUR BRAIN AROUND...

BRAIN OF SOMEONE WHO KNOWS ALL ABOUT TUDOR HISTORY

HENRY VIII HAD A SERVANT OF THE STOOL - HIS JOB WAS TO WIPE HENRY'S BOTTOM

JUST LIKE ME! I'VE GOT A REAR WIPER!

STILL TOO BIG TO GET INSIDE YOUR HEAD? OH, DEAR. THEN LET'S THROW OUT ALL THE BORING BITS AND JUST LEARN THE **HORRIBLE** HISTORY OF TUDOR TIMES. NOW WE HAVE A BRAIN THE SIZE OF A FOOTBALL. A MIGHTY POWERHOUSE OF A BRAIN. A HORRIBLE HISTORIES READER'S BRAIN.

SORRY. I WOULD HAVE TROUBLE FINDING GLASSES TO FIT

I SUPPOSE THAT MEANS ONE THING. FOR ORDINARY READERS WE NEED A HIGH-SPEED HISTORY OF THE TUDORS, DON'T WE? JUST THE HORRIBLE BITS AND THE BITS THAT YOU REALLY WANT TO KNOW?

PERFECT

SO WHAT ARE YOU WAITING FOR?

BATTLING AT BOSWORTH
RICHARD III, HENRY TUDOR AND BOSWORTH FIELD

THE TERRIFYING TUDOR FAMILY RULED ENGLAND, WALES AND IRELAND FOR NEARLY 120 YEARS. THOUSANDS OF PEOPLE DIED. HOW ON EARTH DID THEY GET THEIR BLOODTHIRSTY BUMS ON THE THRONE? I'M GLAD YOU ASKED. IT ALL STARTED WITH KING RICHARD III, WHO WAS NO ANGEL HIMSELF... WELL, MAYBE A HELL'S ANGEL. IT WAS 1483...

SOME WRITERS SAID RICHARD III HAD A TWISTED BODY.

WELL, THEY WOULD SAY THAT ... THEY DIDN'T LIKE ME

YOU **HAVE** GOT A BIT OF A DODGY ARM, SIR

RICHARD'S OLDER BROTHER, KING EDWARD IV, DIED. ED'S SON, EDWARD V, SHOULD HAVE TAKEN THE THRONE. **SHOULD** HAVE.

HAH! I THINK NOT. A TWELVE-YEAR-OLD BOY CAN'T RULE. TELL HIM, WILL SLAUGHTER

YOU CAN'T RULE, LITTLE ED. DEAR UNCLE RICHARD WILL LOOK AFTER THE THRONE TILL YOU'RE OLD ENOUGH. YOU AND YOUR LITTLE BROTHER THE DUKE OF YORK WILL BE CARED FOR

THANKS, UNCLE RICHARD. BUT WHERE WILL WE LIVE?

No one knows for sure what happened to the princes. But one story says King Richard wanted rid of them...

THE BATTLE OF BOSWORTH FIELD BEGAN. RICHARD'S ARMY MARCHED DOWN AMBIEN HILL TO ATTACK HENRY TUDOR'S MEN IN THE MUDDY VALLEY BELOW.

RICHARD LED A CHARGE OF HIS KNIGHTS DOWN THE HILL INTO THE VALLEY. HENRY TUDOR'S FLAG-CARRIER HELD UP THE TUDOR FLAG AND RICHARD CHOPPED OFF HIS ARM.

SWISHH

BUT RICHARD'S HORSE GOT STUCK IN THE MUD AND HE WAS KNOCKED DOWN.

HENRY TUDOR'S MEN HACKED HIM TO DEATH...

THUMP SMACK

AND THEN LORD STANLEY'S ARMY RODE TO HELP ... RODE TO HELP HENRY TUDOR, THAT IS. THE TRAITOR! BUT WHAT ABOUT HIS SON, THE HOSTAGE?

SHAME IF HE DIES ... BUT I HAVE OTHER SONS

YES, HE REALLY SAID THAT. CHARMING, EH?

So the first Tudor, Henry VII, came to the English throne thanks to Lord Stanley's treachery. Two little skeletons HAVE been found buried in the Tower of London. Are they the Princes that Will Slaughter murdered?

Rotten Richard was buried in a stone coffin and placed in a secret grave.

It is said that, years later, the coffin was dug up and used as a horse trough.

Fair enough. Just like a horse with a head down at the trough ... his rein was over.

CLAIMING THE CROWN

HENRY VII, LAMBERT SIMNEL AND PERKIN WARBECK

OH BUT HE WAS A MEAN MAN WAS HENRY VII. HE WAS RUTHLESS ... AND TOOTHLESS TOO. (THE TUDORS ALL SEEMED TO HAVE BAD TEETH.) HE WAS SURE SOMEONE WOULD COME ALONG AND TRY TO THROW HIM OFF THE THRONE. AND THE BIGGEST DANGER WAS FROM EDWARD V AND THE DUKE OF YORK... YES, THAT'S RIGHT, THE TWO PRINCES WHO WERE PROBABLY MURDERED IN THE TOWER OF LONDON. SPOOKY.

THE FIRST PLOT TO OVERTHROW HENRY WAS DREAMED UP BY A PRIEST AND TEACHER CALLED ROGER SYMONS...

I HATE HENRY TUDOR. HATE HIM, HATE HIM, HATE HIM TO BITS.

DID I MENTION THAT I DON'T LIKE HIM?

SNEAKY SYMONS CAME UP WITH A PLOT...

I HAVE A VERY BRIGHT PUPIL CALLED LAMBERT SIMNEL...

RUFFLE

THAT'S ME! BRIGHT AS A BUTTON. CALL ME SUPER SIMNEL

AND THAT'S WHAT THE EARL OF KILDARE DID...

PEOPLE OF IRELAND, I PRESENT TO YOU THE TRUE KING OF ENGLAND AND IRELAND - EDWARD THE SIXTH

HOORAY! BUT...

KING HENRY VII COULD HAVE TOLD THEM...

I HAVE EDWARD OF WARWICK LOCKED IN THE TOWER OF LONDON!

THE REAL EDWARD WAS LET OUT. HE WAS PARADED ROUND THE STREETS OF LONDON. PEOPLE WERE ALLOWED TO VISIT HIM TO SEE LAMBERT WAS A FAKE.

AH, BUT MAYBE THE BOY IN THE TOWER ESCAPED AND YOU ARE THE FAKE

OOOOH! MAYBE I AM!

THE REAL EDWARD OF WARWICK WASN'T VERY BRIGHT.

AND LAMBERT LIVED ON TO A GOOD AGE, WORKING IN THE ROYAL PALACES. BUT HENRY FACED ANOTHER REBEL IN **1498**. THIS ONE WAS CALLED PERKIN WARBECK AND PUTRID PERKIN SAID...

I AM RICHARD, DUKE OF YORK ... THE LITTLE PRINCE FROM THE TOWER ... BUT I ESCAPED

OH, NO, HERE WE GO AGAIN

SHALL WE GIVE HIM A JOB IN THE KITCHENS TOO?

NO, WE ALREADY HAVE A SPIT-TURNER. HANG HIM

I COULD DO THE WASHING UP ... ERK!

YOINK

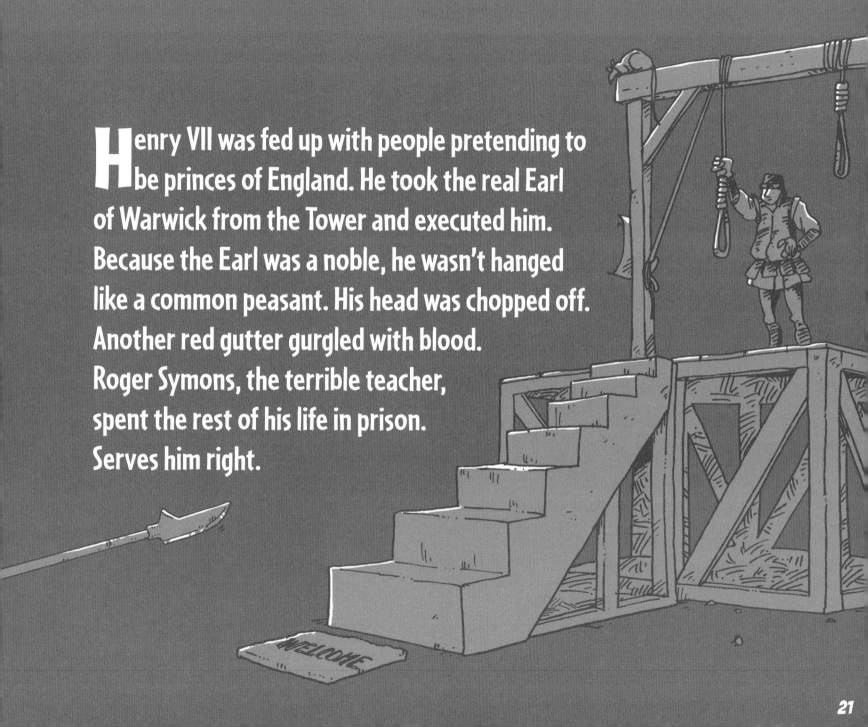

Henry VII was fed up with people pretending to be princes of England. He took the real Earl of Warwick from the Tower and executed him. Because the Earl was a noble, he wasn't hanged like a common peasant. His head was chopped off. Another red gutter gurgled with blood. Roger Symons, the terrible teacher, spent the rest of his life in prison. Serves him right.

HENRY THE HATE-TH

HENRY VIII, FRANCE AND FLODDEN

HENRY VII DIED AND HIS SON HENRY VIII TOOK THE THRONE IN 1509. HENRY VIII WANTED TO BE A GREAT KNIGHT. HE WAS A TALL AND POWERFUL YOUNG MAN AND DID WHAT MANY YOUNG MEN LIKE TO DO … HE SPENT ALL THE MONEY HIS MEAN DAD HAD SAVED. HEN HAD MASSIVE PARTIES, GREAT PALACES AND LOTS OF SERVANTS. BUT THE MOST EXPENSIVE THING OF ALL WAS GOING TO WAR.

KING HENRY VII HAD TWO FINE SONS, PRINCE ARTHUR AND PRINCE HENRY.

ARTHUR, YOU ARE PRINCE OF WALES. ONE DAY, SON, ALL THE REST WILL BE YOURS

Prince Arthur

Prince Henry

THANKS, DAD

GRRRR. I'M ANGRY

AND YOU CAN MARRY PRINCESS CATHERINE OF ARAGON

THANKS, DAD

MUCHAS GRACIAS!

GRRRR! I'M ANGRIER

AFTER FOUR YEARS HENRY WAS RESTLESS...

I'LL USE MY DEAD DAD'S MONEY TO PAY A BIG ARMY. I'M OFF TO ATTACK FRANCE, MY LOVE. I WILL WIN GLORY FOR ENGLAND

OUI! OUI!

WEE-WEE? YES. I SHOULD HAVE GONE BEFORE I PUT MY ARMOUR ON

BUT WHILE HENRY WAS OFF IN FRANCE, LORD SURREY BROUGHT TERRIBLE NEWS TO CATHERINE.

THE FRENCH HAVE SENT AN ARMY TO SCOTLAND. THE FRENCH AND SCOTS ARE INVADING FROM THE NORTH

THEN LET US FIGHT THEM, AMIGO

I MAY BE 70 AND DODDERY AS A DRUNKEN DUCK BUT I FOUGHT AT BOSWORTH FIELD THIRTY YEARS AGO

YOU DID ... BUT YOU FOUGHT ON THE LOSING SIDE, AMIGO

WOBBLE

WOBBLE

FLEX

TWANG

The Lowland Scots had 6-metre pikes they'd never used before.

The hairy Highlanders had their **broadswords.**

Henry was like a spoilt kid. He hated to see Catherine do well. He looked for faults in his wife and he found one. She had a baby girl, Mary, but Henry wanted a son. The kruel king started looking for another wife to give him a boy that would grow up to be the next king of England.

CHAIN PAIN

HENRY VIII, PILGRIMAGE OF GRACE AND ROBERT ASKE

BY 1532 HENRY WAS REALLY FED UP WITH CATHERINE AND WANTED TO MARRY PRETTY YOUNG ANNE BOLEYN. HE NEEDED A DIVORCE. THE POPE, THE HEAD OF THE CATHOLIC CHURCH, REFUSED TO LET HENRY HAVE A DIVORCE. SO HENRY SAID, 'RIGHT! I'LL HAVE A NEW CHURCH. IT WILL BE THE CHURCH OF ENGLAND. I WILL BE THE HEAD AND I WILL GIVE MYSELF A DIVORCE. NO MORE CATHOLICS IN ENGLAND. THAT'LL TEACH YOU, MR DOPEY POPEY.' BUT LOTS OF ENGLISH PEOPLE STILL WANTED TO BE CATHOLICS. PEOPLE LIKE ROBERT ASKE.

ROBERT ASKE, A ONE-EYED LAWYER, BECAME THE LEADER OF THE REBELS. THE REVOLT AGAINST HENRY WAS KNOWN AS THE PILGRIMAGE OF GRACE.

I HAVE WITH ME REBEL LEADER, ROBERT ASKE. SO, ROBERT, HOW DID YOU GET MIXED UP IN THIS?

I WAS JUST PASSING THROUGH LINCOLNSHIRE ON MY WAY HOME TO YORK AND I WAS CAUGHT UP IN IT

WE BE REVOLTING. WOULD A LAWYER GENT LIKE YOU LIKE TO LEAD US?

NOW YOU ASK...

NO, SIR ... YOU ASKE!

BUT NOT EVERYONE IN THE CITY LEARNED FROM THE LESSON. FIFTY YEARS LATER, IN **1586**, A CATHOLIC CALLED MARGARET CLITHEROE LIVED IN YORK.

THE TERRIBLE TUDOR HENRY MAY BE DEAD BUT HIS DREADFUL DAUGHTER ELIZABETH HATES US CATHOLICS JUST AS MUCH

MARGARET WAS CAUGHT HIDING A CATHOLIC PRIEST IN HER HOUSE. SHE WAS TAKEN TO COURT.

DO YOU PLEAD GUILTY OR NOT GUILTY?

NEITHER. IF I PLEAD NOT GUILTY YOU WILL TORTURE MY CHILDREN

MARGARET'S PUNISHMENT WAS ONE OF TUDOR TIMES' MOST TERRIBLE...

YOU WILL BE PRESSED TILL YOU PLEAD

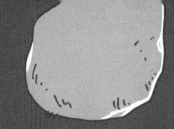
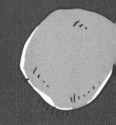

THEY CRUSHED MARGARET'S BODY. THEY COULDN'T CRUSH HER SPIRIT.

MAYBE I SHOULD BECOME A CATHOLIC? THEY'RE REAL HEROES

Robert Aske and Margaret Clitheroe were great Catholic heroes from York. But the MOST famous York rebel was still to come ... a sixteen-year-old boy who may have seen Margaret die. Twenty years later HE became England's most famous Catholic rebel. His name was Guy Fawkes. So Tudor terror just made Catholics stronger.

Catherine of Aragon
Divorced

Anne Boleyn
Beheaded

Jane Seymour
Died

THE *SIX* WIVES OF HENRY VIII

Anne of Cleves
Divorced

Catherine Howard
Beheaded

Catherine Parr
Survived

EDS YOU WIN
EDWARD VI, LIFE AND DEATH

ANNE BOLEYN CAUSED ALL THAT TROUBLE. BUT SHE COULD ONLY GIVE HENRY VIII ANOTHER DAUGHTER - ELIZABETH. HENRY HAD ANNE'S HEAD LOPPED OFF. HENRY'S THIRD WIFE, JANE SEYMOUR, AT LAST GAVE HENRY A SON - THE WEEDY EDWARD ... THEN SHE DIED. HENRY TRIED THREE MORE WIVES - ANNE OF CLEVES (DIVORCED), CATHERINE HOWARD (BEHEADED) AND CATHERINE PARR. THE LAST ONE SURVIVED, AND IT WAS HENRY WHO FINALLY DIED IN **1547**. LITTLE ED TOOK THE THRONE...

47

Mary Tudor - daughter of Catherine Of Aragon, remember - came to the throne. But she was Catholic. Oh, dear, here we go again. Now it's the Catholics' turn to bully the Protestants. One minute it's safe to be a Protestant then it's safe to be a Catholic. Is there any safe thing to be? Yes. Be a carrot.

CHOPPING AND CHANGING

BLOODY MARY AND THE PROTESTANTS

HISTORY CAN BE CRUEL. MARY TUDOR HAS BEEN DEAD **450** YEARS AND HOW DO HISTORY BOOKS REMEMBER HER? AS 'MERRY MARY'? OR 'FAIRY MARY'? NO. SHE IS REMEMBERED AS 'BLOODY MARY'. DOES SHE DESERVE THAT? YOU DECIDE ... AND DECIDE HOW **YOU** WOULD LIKE TO BE REMEMBERED ... GRUESOME GARY OR PIE-FACE POLLY?

52

THERE'S ONLY ONE WAY TO STOP THAT HAPPENING AGAIN FOR JANE. CHOP HER. MAKE SURE JANE GREY SEES HER HUSBAND GO TO HIS EXECUTION FIRST

SO QUEEN MARY SENT HER COUSIN JANE GREY TO HER DEATH

I AM VERY GLAD I AM NO LONGER QUEEN

ME TOO

YOINK

OOOOH! THAT'S A CRUEL TWIST, MAJ

JANE WAS ONLY FIFTEEN AND A TINY GIRL. SHE DIED BRAVELY. SHE SAID...

I am ready and glad to end my woeful days.

BUT HER EXECUTION WAS A JOKE!

54

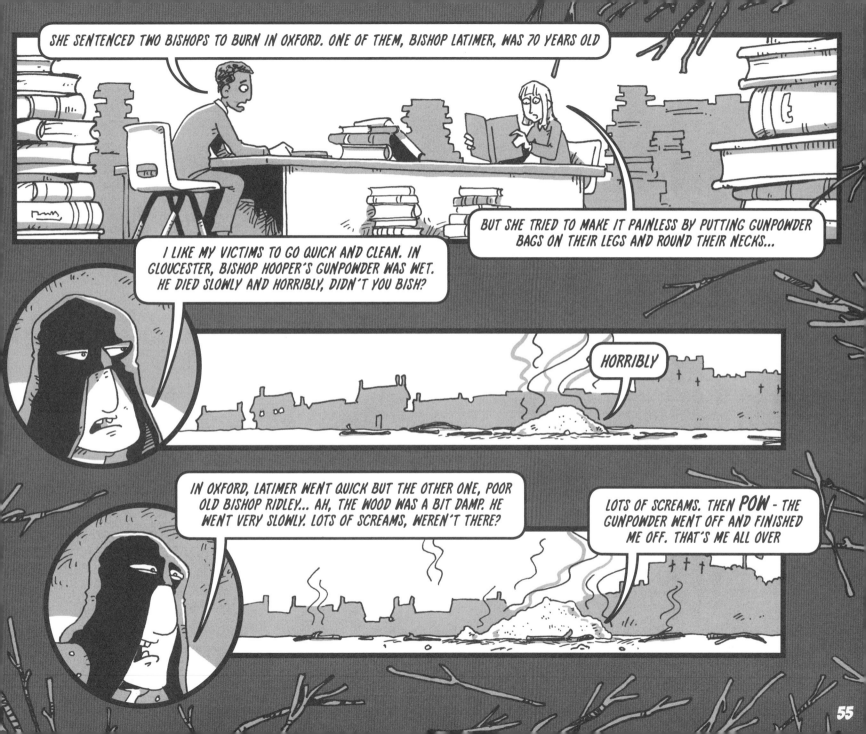

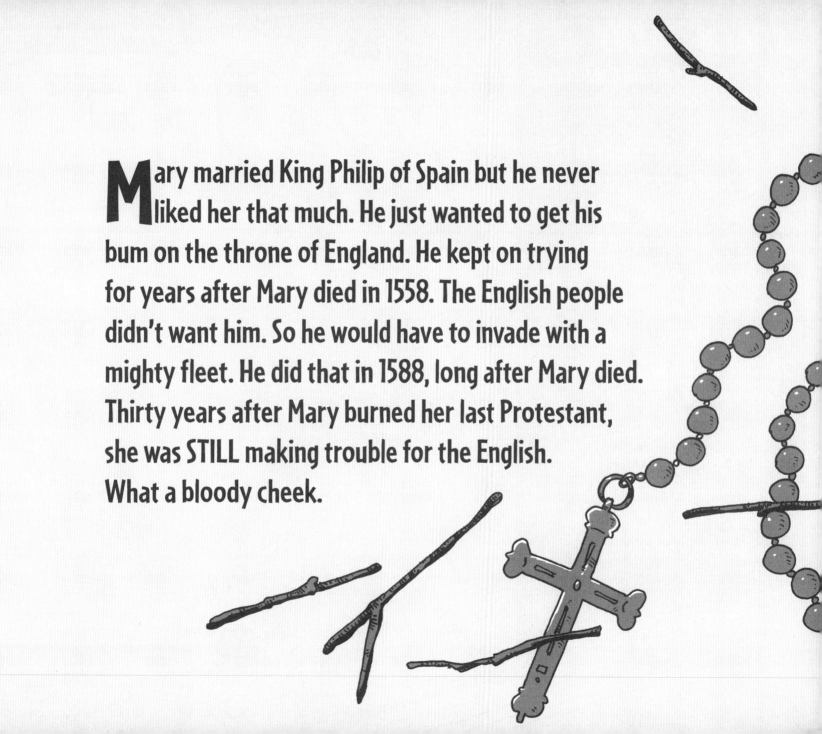

Mary married King Philip of Spain but he never liked her that much. He just wanted to get his bum on the throne of England. He kept on trying for years after Mary died in 1558. The English people didn't want him. So he would have to invade with a mighty fleet. He did that in 1588, long after Mary died. Thirty years after Mary burned her last Protestant, she was STILL making trouble for the English. What a bloody cheek.

SPAIN GAINS
SIR FRANCIS DRAKE AND THE SPANISH ARMADA

WHEN SCARY MARY DIED, HER SISTER ELIZABETH TOOK THE THRONE. LIZZIE WAS THE LAST OF THE TERRIFYING TUDORS AND JUST AS AWFUL AS THE OTHERS. KING PHILIP OF SPAIN STILL FANCIED THE ENGLISH THRONE SO HE SET OFF WITH A MASSIVE FLEET OF SHIPS - THE ARMADA - TO INVADE. FRIZZY LIZZIE COULDN'T STOP HIM ALONE. SHE NEEDED THE HELP OF HER SUPER SAILORS. MEN LIKE SIR FRANCIS DRAKE...

59

DOUGHTY WAS ARRESTED AND SENT TO ONE OF THE SMALLEST SHIPS IN DRAKE'S FLEET. HE MOANED THAT HE HAD NO FOOD OR WATER. THE CREW TOLD HIM...

EEUW!

EAT AND DRINK FROM THE POO BUCKETS WE HAVE ON DECK

NO. POO

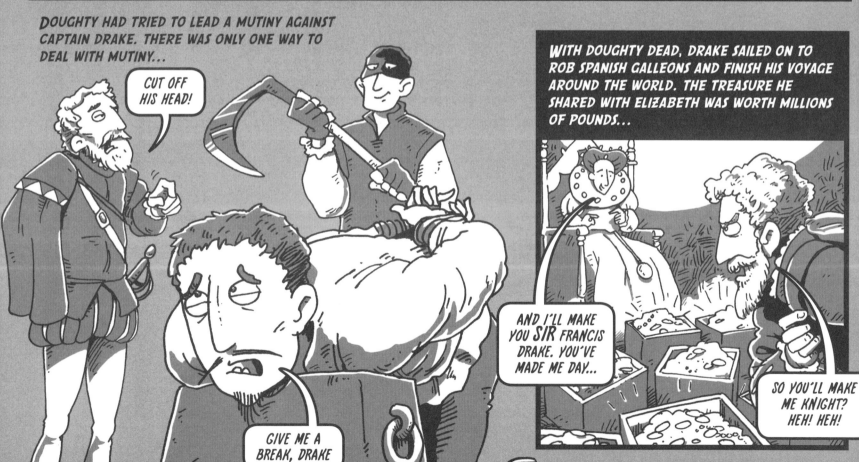

DOUGHTY HAD TRIED TO LEAD A MUTINY AGAINST CAPTAIN DRAKE. THERE WAS ONLY ONE WAY TO DEAL WITH MUTINY...

CUT OFF HIS HEAD!

GIVE ME A BREAK, DRAKE

WITH DOUGHTY DEAD, DRAKE SAILED ON TO ROB SPANISH GALLEONS AND FINISH HIS VOYAGE AROUND THE WORLD. THE TREASURE HE SHARED WITH ELIZABETH WAS WORTH MILLIONS OF POUNDS...

AND I'LL MAKE YOU SIR FRANCIS DRAKE. YOU'VE MADE ME DAY...

SO YOU'LL MAKE ME KNIGHT? HEH! HEH!

THE FAMOUS STORY SAYS DARING DRAKE WAS PLAYING BOWLS AT PLYMOUTH WHEN THE SPANISH FLEET CAME INTO SIGHT...

SIR FRANCIS, OH, SIR FRANCIS ... THE SPANISH FLEET IS OFF THE COAST

THERE IS PLENTY OF TIME TO FINISH THE GAME AND STILL BEAT THE SPANIARDS

DRAKE'S SHIPS SAILED AFTER THE SPANISH. AS IT GREW DARK THE FLEET FOLLOWED A LANTERN ON THE BACK OF DRAKE'S SHIP. THEN DRAKE SPOTTED A RICH GALLEON AND ORDERED...

I WANT TO ROB IT, NOT SINK IT. PUT OUT THE LANTERN SO THE SPANISH WON'T SEE US COMING

DRAKE **DID** CAPTURE THE SPANISH GALLEON. BUT NEXT MORNING...

WHERE'S THE REST OF ME FLEET?

THEY GOT LOST WHEN YOU PUT OUT THE LANTERN

HORRIBLE HISTORIES NOTE:
THE STORY WAS TOLD **37** YEARS AFTER IT WAS SUPPOSED TO HAVE HAPPENED ... SO THE TALE MAY NOT BE TRUE

A STORM HELPED THE LUCKY DUCKY. IT DROVE THE SPANISH INTO THE SHALLOW WATERS NEAR HOLLAND. DRAKE WENT AFTER THEM...

SET FIRE TO SOME OLD SHIPS. LET THE WIND CARRY THEM INTO THE SPANISH FLEET

NOT A GOOD IDEA

THE INVASION WAS OVER. BUT, IN ENGLAND, QUEEN LIZ DIDN'T KNOW THAT. SHE WAITED WITH HER TROOPS. SHE WAS SUPPOSED TO HAVE MADE A FAMOUS SPEECH...

I may have the body of a weak and feeble woman, but I have the heart and stomach of a king.

I HOPE THE KING DOESN'T WANT THEM BACK!

LIKE THE BOWLS STORY, THIS WAS TOLD MANY YEARS LATER. MAYBE SHE NEVER SAID IT AT ALL.

A YEAR AFTER THE ARMADA WAS BEATEN...

NOW, DUCKY, I WANT YOU TO GO TO SPAIN AND SINK THE REST OF THEIR SHIPS

GREAT DRAKE WILL MAKE THE SPANISH SHAKE AND QUAKE

MANY SPANISH SHIPS BURNED, THE REST WERE SCATTERED.

BUT IT WAS A BIT OF A DISASTER.

I RECKON WE LOST 10,000 MEN AND 20 SHIPS, SIR

EVEN A DRAKE CAN MAKE A MISTAKE

SO DRAKE SET OFF TO ROB GALLEONS OFF THE COAST OF SOUTH AMERICA – THE AREA KNOWN AS THE SPANISH MAIN. BUT THIS TIME THE SPANISH WERE READY AND WAITING. HE LOST BATTLE AFTER BATTLE.

THE PAIN IN SPAIN LIES MAINLY IN THE MAIN

BUT IT WASN'T A SPANISH BULLET OR CANNONBALL THAT KILLED HIM IN **1594**. IT WAS A DISEASE CALLED DYSENTERY – SWEAT, SICKNESS, RUNNY POO, THEN DEATH. HE WAS THROWN OVER THE SIDE OF HIS SHIP – BURIED AT SEA.

IT'S FISH-CAKE DRAKE

Elizabeth didn't just want Spanish gold. She also discovered that selling African prisoners in America made her sailors a lot of money. Money that she shared. She had started the slave trade. It would bring misery to millions for over two hundred years. Drake was deadly, but the last Tudor queen was far more cruel. Drake had Doughty's head cut off. But Queen Liz had hundreds of people executed ... and one of them was her own cousin.

Mary executed her cousin too, remember. Seems to have been the Tudors' horrible hobby.

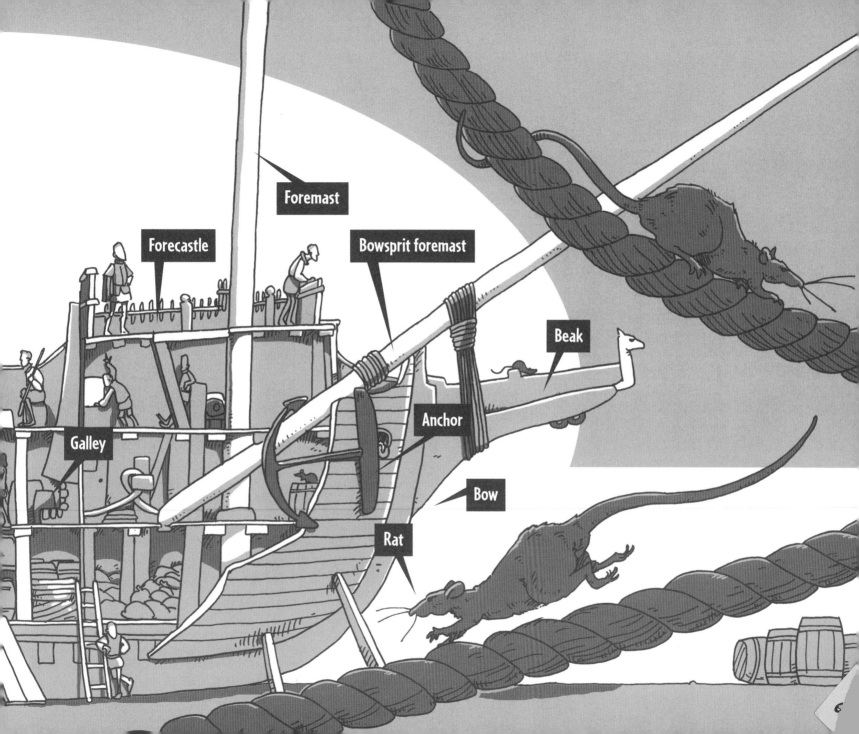

QUEEN of CHOPS
MARY QUEEN OF SCOTS

THE TUDORS DIDN'T JUST RULE IN ENGLAND. HENRY VIII'S SISTER, MARGARET, BECAME QUEEN OF SCOTLAND. HER SON, JAMES V, BECAME KING TILL HE LOST A BATTLE AGAINST THE ENGLISH IN **1542**. HE DIED OF A BROKEN HEART SOON AFTER. THAT MEANT JAMES'S DAUGHTER, MARY QUEEN OF SCOTS, BECAME QUEEN. SHE WAS SIX DAYS OLD AT THE TIME. WHAT A START TO HER LIFE ... AND WHAT AN END.

HENRY VIII

MARGARET TUDOR

KING JAMES IV of SCOTLAND

MARY of GUISE

JAMES V

MARY ~ QUEEN OF SCOTS

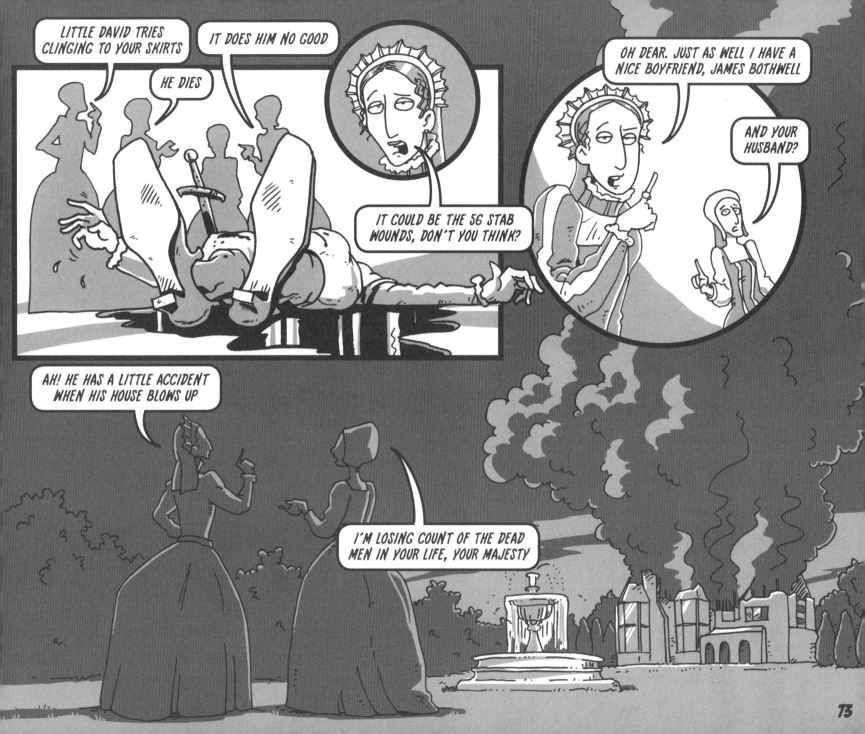

74

Mary
M suffered
a death as horrible
and bungled as John Huntly's.
It took three chops and a bit of sawing to remove her head. When the executioner bent to pick up the head he grasped it by the hair. No one told him Mary wore a wig. The head fell out and bounced across the platform. Now THAT'S Horrible History.
Yet again someone died a dreadful death so a Tudor could stay on the throne.

PLAYS AND PIGEONS

THEATRE, PLAGUES AND CURES

LIFE FOR QUEEN LIZ WASN'T ALL ABOUT BEING CRUEL TO CATHOLICS AND COUSINS. SOMETIMES SHE LIKED TO GET AWAY FROM THE MURDER, THE HORROR AND THE BLOODSHED. QUEEN LIZ ENJOYED THE THEATRE WHERE, FOR A CHANGE, SHE COULD WATCH WONDERFUL PLAYS ... ABOUT MURDER, HORROR AND BLOODSHED. PLAYS BY CLEVER WRITERS LIKE WILLIAM SHAKESPEARE.

SHAKESPEARE LIVED IN VIOLENT TIMES, SO MANY OF HIS PLAYS WERE PRETTY VIOLENT TOO. TAKE 'TITUS ANDRONICUS'. A HORRIBLY HISTORICAL PLAY. IT WAS SET IN ROME AND STARTED WITH TITUS MAKING A HUMAN SACRIFICE - THE SON OF TAMORA.

TAKE YOUNG ALARBUS TO THE ALTAR, CUT HIM INTO PIECES THEN BURN HIM AS A SACRIFICE TO MY DEAD SONS

THAT'S NOT VERY FAIR, MUM!

I TOLD HIM THAT, SON, BUT THE OLD FOOL WON'T LISTEN

BUT TITUS'S DAUGHTER, LAVINIA, IS THE REAL LOSER. SHE OVERHEARS A REVENGE PLOT TO KILL TITUS. THE PLOTTERS HAVE TO SILENCE HER...

YOU CAN'T STOP HER, AARON

OH YES I CAN!

I'M GOING TO TELL, AND YOU CAN'T KILL ME COS I'M AN UNARMED WOMAN. TELL HIM, TAMORA

BUT RUNNING AWAY WAS THE ONLY REAL ANSWER...

TO FLEE OR NOT TO FLEE, THAT IS THE QUESTION

People died, but Liz the last Tudor lived on. The problem was she was too old and tired to rule the country. She wouldn't say who would rule once she was dead. The Queen had no children and had never married. But she liked young men. Maybe a young lord could marry her and, when she hopped the twig, England would have a strong young king.
Maybe...

MY BEST PLAGUE CURES

* SWALLOW POWDERED HUMAN SKULL

* EAT LIVE SPIDERS
(COVERED IN BUTTER TO MAKE THEM SLIDE DOWN A LITTLE EASIER)

* FUSTIGATION
(THE PATIENT IS GIVEN A GOOD BEATING)

BOK

LIZ THE LAST

ELIZABETH, ESSEX AND SHAKESPEARE

BY 1600 ELIZABETH WAS OLD. HER TEETH WERE BLACK AND ROTTEN – SHE LIKED EATING MARZIPAN BUT NEVER CLEANED HER TEETH. HER HAIR WAS FALLING OUT SO SHE WORE GINGER WIGS. HER WRINKLED FACE WAS PAINTED SMOOTH WITH WHITE MAKE-UP. SHE HAD JUST FOUR BATHS A YEAR AND PROBABLY SMELLED LIKE A DEAD CAT IN A JEWELLED GOWN. NO MAN WOULD FANCY THIS FREAK WITH A FACE LIKE A PAINTED PIE-CRUST, WOULD THEY?

THE DUKE OF ESSEX DID ... OR SAID HE DID

I NEVER SAW TRUE BEAUTY TILL THIS NIGHT

HMMMM! I THINK MY FRIEND SHAKESPEARE WROTE THAT LINE IN 'ROMEO AND JULIET'

AH ... MAYBE ... BUT HE MUST HAVE BEEN THINKING OF YOUR BEAUTIFUL MAJESTY WHEN HE WROTE IT

YOU ARE TOO CHEEKY, MY LORD ESSEX... I'LL GIVE YOU THREE HOURS TO STOP YOUR NONSENSE

YOU KNOW THAT, MY EVIL FRIEND, BUT OLD LIZ DOESN'T. WRITE A LETTER TO LIZ...

HERE YOU ARE...

My Gracious Queen

My spies have heard that your Doctor, Roderigo Lopez, has been paid by his Spanish masters to poison you. Lopez, as you know, is Jewish. Jews are not popular and you would be _most_ popular if you had him executed.

I hope I have saved your life with this news.

Your most humble servant

Essex

THE QUEEN'S SPY-MASTERS QUESTIONED ALL THE SPANISH SPIES THEY COULD FIND TO UNCOVER THE TRUTH. SHE WAS FURIOUS ... WITH ESSEX.

My Lord Essex

I have looked into your claims against Doctor Lopez. It seems the man is innocent. Your spies are fools... and so is their master.

Do not bother me with this matter again.

Elisabeth

ER

THEN HE HAD ANOTHER IDEA... ESSEX HAD ALL THE PEOPLE LOPEZ WORKED WITH BROUGHT TO HIS DUNGEONS...

LOPEZ IS PLOTTING TO POISON THE QUEEN, ISN'T HE?

NO!

ELIZABETH HAD TO BELIEVE ESSEX'S STORY NOW. THE POOR DOCTOR LOPEZ WAS SENT TO THE SCAFFOLD WHERE HE DIED A TRAITOR'S DEATH. HE WAS HANGED TILL HALF-DEAD, CUT OPEN AND HAD HIS BOWELS RIPPED OUT, THEN HE WAS BEHEADED AND CUT INTO QUARTERS.

EVEN SHAKESPEARE CASHED IN ON THE HATRED OF JEWS BY WRITING A PLAY WITH A JEWISH VILLAIN, 'THE MERCHANT OF VENICE'. IT WAS A HUGE SUCCESS ... EXCEPT WITH THE SUFFERING JEWS, OF COURSE.

I WANT A POUND OF HIS FLESH, CUT OFF FROM NEAR HIS HEART

BOO!

BOO!

BUT THE EVIL ESSEX TRICK WORKED AND ELIZABETH FORGAVE HIM ... THIS TIME.

NOW IT'S TIME I TOOK OVER THE THRONE

OOOOH! SHE WON'T LIKE THAT

SURE ENOUGH THE QUEEN BANISHED ESSEX. HE DECIDED TO PLOT A REBELLION. HE TURNED TO WILLIAM SHAKESPEARE TO HELP...

MY FRIENDS ARE COMING TO MY HOUSE. I WILL PAY YOU FORTY POUNDS TO PERFORM YOUR PLAY, 'RICHARD II'

WHAT? BUT THAT'S A PLAY ABOUT A REBELLION. THE QUEEN HAS BANNED IT

FORTY POUNDS, SHAKEY. IT'S WORTH THE RISK

SHAKESPEARE WENT FREE. BUT ELIZABETH'S CHOPPING DAYS WERE OVER.

I'VE BEHEADED MY COUSIN, MY DOCTOR AND NOW MY FAVOURITE MAN

THAT'S WHAT YOU TUDORS DO BEST, YOUR HIGHNESS

IN TWO YEARS ELIZABETH WAS ILL AND RAVING. SHE WANDERED ROUND HER PALACE WITH A RUSTY SWORD...

THEY'RE OUT TO GET ME! I'LL FIGHT YOU ALL. COME ON, FIGHT, YOU COWARDS

THE LAST TUDOR WENT THE WAY THE FIRST TUDOR HAD ARRIVED. WAVING A SWORD. SHE DIED ON 24 MARCH 1603. THE LAST OF THE TRULY TERRIBLE TUDORS.

SO WHO GETS THE THRONE NOW?

KING JAMES OF SCOTLAND ... THE SON OF MARY QUEEN OF SCOTS. THE WOMAN ELIZABETH HAD EXECUTED

IT'S A FUNNY OLD WORLD, ISN'T IT?

94

There had been years of famine in which poor people had died on the streets or fed their children on cats, dogs and nettle roots. So no one was really unhappy to see the last of the Tudors turn up her toes and die.

LOOK OUT
FOR
KNIGHTS
A HIGH-SPEED HISTORY

TERRY DEARY

ILLUSTRATED BY
DAVE SMITH